GIG

by the same author

FRINCK, A LIFE IN THE DAY OF and
SUMMER WITH MONIKA (novel and poems)

WATCHWORDS (poems)

AFTER THE MERRYMAKING (poems)

OUT OF SEQUENCE (poems)

SPORTING RELATIONS (poems)

IN THE GLASSROOM (poems)

GIG

Roger McGough

Jonathan Cape Thirty Bedford Square London

First published 1973

Reprinted 1974, 1977

© 1973 by Roger McGough

JONATHAN CAPE LTD, 30 BEDFORD SQUARE, LONDON WCI

ISBN Hardback 0 224 00921 4
     Paperback 0 224 00924 9

The following poems were first published in a limited edition by
Turret Books, 1972: 'George and the Dragonfly',
'Out of Sequence', 'Vampire', 'Tightrope', 'Warlock Poems',
'The Most Unforgettable Character I've Ever Met Gives Advice
to the Young Poet', 'Humdinger', 'Tigerdreams', 'The Picture'.

'Out of Sequence' was also published in *The House That
Jack Built*, Allen & Unwin, 1973.

'Birmingham' and 'Newcastle' were published in *The Little
Word Machine*, 1972.

PRINTED PHOTOLITHO AND BOUND IN GREAT BRITAIN
BY EBENEZER BAYLIS AND SON, LIMITED
THE TRINITY PRESS, WORCESTER, AND LONDON

Contents

I ON THE ROAD

Huddersfield 11
Birmingham 12
Wolverhampton 14
Canterbury 15
Canterbury 16
Brighton .17
Newcastle 19
Bradford 20
Bradford 21
Bradford 23
Leeds 24
Sheffield 26
Loughborough 27
Nottingham 29
Cardiff 30
Cardiff 6 p.m. 32
Cardiff 11 a.m. 33
epilogue (or cosy biscuit) 34

II AT THE ROADSIDE

George and the dragonfly 37
ofa sunday 38
crusader 39
warlock poems (i), (ii), (iii) 40
vampire 43
tigerdreams 44
tightrope 45
humdinger 46
exsomnia 47
bravado 48
un 49
happiness 50

the picture 51
the power of poets 52
the most unforgettable character i've ever met gives
  advice to the young poet 53
the identification 55
out of sequence 57
tailpiece 59

I ON THE ROAD

LIFE ON THE ROAD WITH ONE OF TODAYS
SUPERGROUPS.
WHAT ITS LIKE FROM THE INSIDE.
A NO-HOLDS-BARRED STORY OF LOVE-HUNGRY
YOUNGMEN AND THE GIRLS THEY MEET.
THE LESBIANS, THE PLASTERCASTERS, THE
GROUPIES OUT FOR THRILLS.
THE WEIRDOS, THE JUNKIES AND THE PERVERTS.
GANGBANGS. ORGIES IN THE VAN.
EXCITEMENT ... ECSTASY ... SEXUAL
DELINQUENCY ... THERES NO BUSINESS LIKE ...

Huddersfield

Monster cooling towers stand guard
lest the town takes to the hills,
4 p.m. and the sky the colour of frozen lard.

Secondhand soap in my little B and B.
My only comfort, the Kozeeglow hotwaterbottle,
provided free of charge by the management
after November 15 (Remember to screw tightly).
'Could I please have a front door key?'
I ask the man on my way out.
'You won't need one' he replies,
'We don't lock up till midnight.'
I explain that being a traveller
in ladies' nighties, my work keeps me
out until the early hours. He winks
and lends me his own, personal,
oneandonly, private, worthitsweight
in gold, magic, back door key.

Later, having not taken Huddersfield Polytechnic
by storm, we retire to the Punjab
to lick our wounds and dangle our disappointment
in the curry. Chicken with 2 chapatis.
Home cooking. The real McCoy sahib.
Outside, no one on the tundrastreets
save we eternal action seekers.
Too full to drink, too cold to laugh.
At one a.m. we give up the ghost
town and steam back to the gaff.

in bed I wear socks and my grey woolly hat,
shiver, and regret not having filled the Kozeeglow
with vindaloo.

Birmingham

Auschwitz with H and C
Seven a.m. and vacuum cleaners
at full throttle. Brum Brum Brum.
Grey curtains against a grey sky
Wall to wall linoleum and the
ashtray nailed to the mantelpiece.
Sacrificing breakfast for semidreams
I remember the days we stayed
at the Albany. Five Ten a night.
I was somebody then (the one on the right
with glasses singing Lily the Pink).
The Dolce Vita.

At 10. o'clock the Kommodante
(a thin spinster, prim as shrapnel)
balls me out of bed. 'Get up
or I'll fetch the police. Got guests
arriving at midday. Businessmen.
This rooms to be cleaned and ready.'
  i Kleenextissues to be uncrumpled and ironed
 ii Dust reassembled
iii Fresh nail in the ashtray
 iv Harpic down the plughole
  v Beds to be seen and not aired.

In the lounge my fellow refugees
are cowering together for warmth.
𝕹𝖔 𝖌𝖆𝖘 𝖋𝖎𝖗𝖊𝖘 𝖆𝖑𝖑𝖔𝖜𝖊𝖉 𝖇𝖊𝖋𝖔𝖗𝖊 6.30
𝖎𝖓 𝖙𝖍𝖊 𝖊𝖛𝖊𝖓𝖎𝖓𝖌.   𝖁𝖊𝖗𝖇𝖔𝖙𝖊𝖓.
We draw straws. The loser
rings the service bell. 'Tea! Tea!!
I've got more to do than run round
making tea at all hours of the day.

Tea!!!' She goosesteps down the hall.
A strange quirk of feet.
When the bill comes there is
included a 12½% service charge.
We tell her to stick it
up her brum. La dolce vita.

Wolverhampton

spiders are holding their wintersports
in the bathroom. Skating on the
lino, skiing down the slippery
slopes of the bath. Burdened
with my British sense of fairplay
and love of animals, I shower
on tiptoe, water at half-throttle.
I try whistling a happy toon.
The walls, painted in memory
of some longdead canary have
cloth ears: grey cunard towels
folded frayed-side in. Outside
the town too is taking an
evening shower before going out
for the night. Less sensitive
than I to the creepycrawlies
creepingcrawling round its aching feet.

Canterbury

in the no mans land
between opening hours
2 winos
compose a pietà

one
asleep on a bench
half bottle of richruby
warm and safe
in his richruby
winepocket

the other
keeping an eye
on the cathedral.

Canterbury

'Its like bashing your head against a brick wall'
sighed the bishop,
bashing my head against a brick wall.
'Five to nine already
and no sign of the cross.'

Brighton

A day to be reckoned with
an indian summer
   indian bluesky
   feathery clouds

A cowboy

blustery cowboy wind
10 gallon sun.

Sitting on the beach minding my own
sandwiches. Scratching your name
on every pebble within reach.

Then leaving the sea to stew
in its own juice, I head
for the hinderland and find
that the only people who say hello
want money.

e.g. The whelkeyed Scottish poet pretender
    (leader of a little band of sand dwellers)
    in return for 5p, wishing me
    peaceandlove, blowing kisses, and
    laughing up his mainline.

e.g. Like an absentminded schoolmaster
    whose class has gone missing on a daytrip
    betweeded and spectacled
    he calls me aside:
    'Irish sir, and gone in the head.'
    He shows me the scars on his scalp.
    'The war sir, Jaze, I'd never fight again,
    not for no one sir. 10 pence would see me right.'
    I saw him right,
    and left.

Deciding to spend some money before I gave it all away
I enter the nearest cafe and browse through the menu.

CRAB SANDWICH 20p
I picture a whole live crab
writhing between two chunks
of fresh bread. Tuck in quick
before it sidles off the plate.
Snap off the pincers first
(use them as toothpicks later).
Now crunch through the shell,
good for the teeth.
Feel the flesh
moist and fibrous.
Chew slowly.
Wash down with hot, sweet
TEA 5p

Newcastle

All night
ghosts of ducks
longsince plucked
waddled menacingly
across the eiderdown.

in the morning
mealyeyed I stood
on the foot of the bed.
The bed yowled
and kicked me across the room.

I picked myself up
and took myself out for a walk
(unfortunately we became separated
so I had to come home alone).

Bradford

The occasional curry

keeps

the

stomach

on

its

toes

Bradford

Saris billow in the wind like dhows off the shore
bus drivers whistle ragas above the traffic roar.
Late afternoon, and darkness already
elbowing its way through the crowded streets.
The pavements glister and are cold.
A lady, brittle with age, teeters along,
keeping balance with a shopping bag
in one hand and a giant box of cornflakes
in the other. Lovers arminarm home
to hot soup and a bath-for-two
Everyone a passer-by or a passer-through.

Up at the university lectures are over for the day,
and students, ruddy
with learning, race back to the digs
to plan revolutions to end revolutions.

When asked why he had elected
to pursue mathematics in academic
seclusion, the old prof had answered:
'because there's safety in numbers.'

Happy show.
Good to see the frontrow getting stoned
on the joint full of herbal tobacco
Mike hands out during his song.
And afterwards its beer out of plastic mugs
then off to the Pennyfarthing
for pie and peas and dances
with the lovelylady with the biggest
tits
east of the pennines (who turns
out later to be a complete ego-
tist
i.e. because she wasn't interested in ME).

Hours later

alone

the failed reveller

wends his wary way

home

No wind

No people

No cars.

Sheets of ice

are nailed

to the streets,

with stars.

Bradford

Knocked up after three hours sleep
'Your seven o'clock call sir'
With Pavlovian urgency I respond and
start dressing, guilty of staying in bed,
terrified of being late, then the truth
hits me like a snowball. No call.
I hadn't ordered an early morning call.
Its a mistake, a joke, I collapse
back into bed and dream of hot pies
thundering down motorways flanked
by huge tits. Its eleven o'clock
and waking to find myself still alive
I get up and go downstairs to celebrate.
The girl at reception calls me over
'The morning papers you ordered sir'
and hands me the Times, Guardian,
Telegraph, Express, Mail, Sun, Mirror,
three copies of the Yorkshire Post and the Beano.
'I didn't order these' I quibble.
'Its written down' says she. And so it is,
in handwriting not my own. A joke.
I accept the Beano. On such a day
as this threatens to be who needs news.

Leeds

1 a.m.

alone
and the ale
wearing off
so quiet
i can hear
the eggs
shuffling

2 a.m.

i don't miss
my teddybear
only you

two hands
where its hot
in a bed
made for two

7 a.m.

alarmclock
sends fireengines
clanging into
my dreams

bedroom is cold

i reach out
and put on
my hangover

8 a.m.

rain crackles
the flags
i pour
whiskey
over my
cornflakes

moonshine breakfast

Sheffield

Sometimes I dont smell so good.
Its not that I dont care about
personal hygiene. I do. Its just that
sometimes the body catches up on me.
Like when Im out all day and
refuse to pay for a wash and
brush up at the local municipal
on lack of principle. And hiding
away in some unfamiliar un
kempt saloon I console myself
theres no such thing as *bad* breath.
All breath is good. And sweat
means the body functions as it
should. I drink my bitter.
Put a pork pie to the knife.
Far sweeter than the stink of
death, is the stink of life.

Loughborough

It seems unlikely now
that I shall ever nod in
the winning goal for Everton
and run around Wembley with the cup.

Unlikely too
that I shall rout
the Aussies at Lords
with my deadly inswingers

that I shall play
the romantic lead in a Hollywood film
based on the Broadway musical
in which I starred

that I shall be a missionary
spreading wisdom
and the Word of God
amongst our pagan bretheren

it all seems unlikely now
and so I seek dreams more mundane
ambitions more easily attained
    a day at the seaside
    a poem started
    a change of beard
    an unruly orgasm
    a new tracksuit

and at the end of each day
I count my successes
(adding 10 if I go to bed sober)

by thus keeping one pace ahead of myself
I need never catch up with the truth

It seems unlikely now
that you will enter this room
close the curtains
and turn back the clock.

Nottingham

Stoned and lonely in the union bar
Looking for a warm student
to fall upon. Someone gentle
and undemanding. History perhaps?
Not Maths or English.

Not English. I'm in
no mood to be laid
alongside our literary heritage
allocated my place in her
golden treasury of flesh.

Geography might do the job.
To snuggle up to
shifting continents and
ocean currents. Swap tonnage
and compare monsoons.

Even Chemistry. Someone
tangible. Flasks, bubblings
and a low flame underneath.
With someone warm like this
I'd take my chances.

Maths would find in me no questions
English Lit. no answers.

Cardiff

and Cardiffs a tart with a heart of gold.
Has been for me since the Poetry Conference
back in sixty-something. All the stars
of the silver page were there. Heroes.
To kiss the mistress of the man
you actually wrote an essay about.
To see huddled in flesh and blood
the bard you thought died in the '30s.
The lecturing, the hectoring, the theorizing,
the self-opinionizing, the factions and the jealousies.
And I took my poems to a party
and nobody asked me to read.
Except Sue, afterwards. Sue, a predipped
velveteenager. Archangelhaired and greeneyed
freeschooled and freeloving who taught me
more about poetry than any conference.

aNd tripPING tHe luMP fanTASTic with bRIan.
Spending two hours in Woolworths
just looking. Then going to the park
and listening to flowers gossiping
                          Then
the comedown.
(stoned out of his head, the captain
has left the bridge. Out of control
the vessel drifts toward uncertain disaster.
Shipwrecked on an iceberg of frozen sugar.)
Watching a drunk staggering
and i am the drunk. Out of sync.
Afraid of what the trafficlights might think.
Lying in bed and becoming my own heartbeat.
The monster fingers on my thighs are my own
tapping out an urgent message only they understand.
When you fall out of love with it
the body can be a foul piece of meat.

Quartered at the Park Hotel.
Well-hung and drawn from all over.
3 star accommo and all expenses paid.
Hospitality is a red rag to a writer.
Brings out the beast. The muse
is bound, gagged and locked in the closet.
Then the pillaging begins. Poetic Licentiousness.
Shoes down the lift-shaft
and chambertin for breakfast.
Naked ladies in corridors
and dirty songs in the lounge.
'Give me football hooligans everytime'
beefs the Night porter to the Day.
'Poets? scruffs more like,
(Except for that nice Mr Macbeth)
Coloured too, some of them.
Whoever heard of coloured poets?'

Cardiff 6 p.m.

No. 12 a long room built under the eaves. Tri-
angular. Like living in a giant Toblerone packet.
One-bar electric fire and a meter only takes
threepenny bits. Sore throat and a cold a comin
sure as eggs is eggs is eggs.
Somewhere between here and London
the van has broken down. No band.
No props. It's going to be a fun show
at the Barry Memorial Hall.
'Drink Brains' says the advert on a beermat.
They'd drink anything down here.
Must be the coaldust and all that
choirpractise. Outside its raining oldwomen
and walkingsticks. The pillow feels damp.
Tears of the previous paying guest.
The eskimos in the room next door
speak fluent welsh at the tops
of their voices. Not a drink to be had
T.B. or not T.B. that is the question.
Pneumonia at least. Sure as eggs
is eggs is eggs is eggs is eggs
is eggs is eggs is eggs is eggs
is eggs croeso is eggs is eggs
is eggs is eggs is eggs is eggs
is eggs is eggs is eggs is eggs

Cardiff 11 a.m.

Down first for breakfast
in the neat and nic-nac tidy
diningroom I am left to my devices.
I pick up cold steel talons
and tear into the heart of Egg
which bleeds over strips of danish
vagina marinated in brine.
Grey shabby Mushrooms squeal
as they are hacked to death
slithering in their own sweat.
Like policemen to a motorway accident,
Toast Arrives. The debris is mopped up.
Nothing remains of the slaughter.
John comes in with Judy.
'Mornin'
'Mornin'
'Up early then?'
'Aye'
Life goes on.

epilogue (or cosy biscuit)

What I wouldn't give for a nine to five.
Biscuits in the right hand drawer,
teabreaks, and typists to mentally undress.

The same faces. Somewhere to hang
your hat and shake your umbrella.
Cosy. Everything in its place.

Upgraded every few years. Hobbies.
Glass of beer at lunchtime
Pension to look forward to.

Two kids. Homeloving wife.
Bit on the side when the occasion arises
H.P. Nothing fancy. Neat semi.

* * *

What I wouldn't give for a nine to five.
Glass of beer in the right hand drawer
H.P. on everything at lunchtime.

The same 2 kids. Somewhere to hang
your wife and shake your bit on the side.
Teabreaks and a pension to mentally undress.

The same semifaces upgraded.
Hobbies every few years, neat typists
in wet macs when the umbrella arises.

What I wouldn't give for a cosy biscuit.

II AT THE ROADSIDE

George and the dragonfly

Georgie Jennings was spit almighty.
When the golly was good
he could down a dragonfly at 30 feet
and drown a 100 midges with the fallout.
At the drop of a cap
he would outspit lads
years older and twice his size.
Freckled and rather frail
he assumed the quiet dignity
beloved of schoolboy heroes.

But though a legend in his own playtime
Georgie Jennings failed miserably in the classroom
and left school at 15 to work for his father.
And talents such as spitting
are considered unbefitting
for upandcoming porkbutchers.

I haven't seen him since,
but like to imagine some summer soiree
when, after a day moistening mince,
George and his wife entertain tanned friends.
and after dinner, sherrytongued talk
drifts back to schooldays
The faces halfrecalled, the adventures
overexaggerated. And the next thing
that shy sharpshooter of days gone by
is led, vainly protesting, on to the lawn
where, in the hush of a golden august evening
a reputation, 20 years tall, is put to the test.
So he takes extra care as yesterheroes must,
fires, and a dragonfly, encapsulated, bites the dust.
Then amidst bravos and tinkled applause,
blushing, Georgie leads them back indoors.

ofa sunday

ofa sunday
the only thing
i burn
at both ends
is my bacon.
Like the tele
phone i am
off the hook

i watch the
newspapers for
hours & browse
through T.V.
miss mass
and wonder
if mass
misses me

crusader

in bed
like a dead
crusader

arms a
cross my chest
i lie

eyes closed
listening
to the bodys glib mechanics

      *   *   *

on the street
outside
men of violence

quarrel.
Their drunken voices
dark weals

on the
glistening
back of the night.

warlock poems

(i)

         when i fly |
         i keepclose
      to chimneystacks and
      gutted warehouses

hovering

         just out of
     reach of men's anger
        i take off
       from bombed-
      sites and model
       my tech-
      nique on litter

              caught

          in |

     the

   wind.
(During the day i camouflage myself
    to blend against a thousand backgrounds | ,
all grey)

         my fear
      is that one morn-
    ing when i have landed
        to re-
      fuel with sadness
        They
      will capture me
       tie my wings
      behind my back
and drive a stake through my | fuselage

(ii)

on a clear night
some
stoned home re-
turner hearing a
cry, might gaze
upwards and see
me silhouett-
ed against the sky
trying vain
ly to get out
through the circular silver escape hatch

(iii)
i saw
      the hearse
           coming towards me
      it was
         too late
             to turn   back
         when it
             drew level
                the coffin
shuddered
      and the bearers
         had greatest
      difficulty   in keeping
            it under control
        the crowd
           turned
              and saw me hiding
they pointed
      and shouted
         and screamed
i took to the air   everything
        was black
           and purple
       except
        the white faces
           advancing

vampire

Blood is an acquired taste
'tis warm and sickly
and sticks to the teeth
a surfeit makes me puke.
I judge my victims as a connoisseur
a sip here, a mouthful there.
I never kill
and am careful to cause no pain
to those who sleeping nourish me
and calling once I never call again.

So if one morning you awake,
stretch, and remember
dark dreams of
               falling
                falling
if your neck is sore
a mark that wasn't there the night before
be not afeared 'tis but a sign
i give thee thanks
i have drunk thy wine.

tigerdreams

i go to sleep on all fours
ready to pounce
on any dream
in which you might appear
Claws withdrawn
i want you live
the image fresh as meat
i want you live
the memories flesh to eat
Every nightmare its the same
prowling through forests
growling your name
until the alarmclock cracks the first twig
and lifting the blankets
i collapse
into the undergrowth.

tightrope

at 7.55 this morning
the circus ran away to join me

there is a lion in the wardrobe
and in the pantry
the clown
goes
    down
           on the bareback rider

the seal in the bath is wearing my hat
and the elephants
have shat on the cat on the mat

my wife (always a dwarf at heart)
juggles naked for the ringmaster
who lashes her approvingly

i stagger out of bed
to shew the tightropewalkers
a thing or two.

humdinger

there's not a one

                            no one
                           anywhere/place

quite like you

i would follow you to the very ends
of our street

                         and often do

(discreet-
ly)

                         onallfours

youra   HUMDINGER

Why, everybody says so

what i wouldn't give for an excursion into your darkest africa.

exsomnia

in bed
counting sheep
my attention
distracted by
a passing nude
when suddenly
a hoof
caught me
on the head
with a soft moan I collapsed

now i lie
by the bed
side more dead
than alive
waiting for the
somnambulance
to arrive

bravado

and you still havent ironed
the trousers of my s.s. uni
form. The baby you say
will grow to love a new
father. Someone will come
and do my job properly.
Someone not closed.

beneath the sheets
i pick my nails
and flick
dirtpellets
soundlessly
into the darkness.
Bravado.

un

the baby
fourteen months
to the month
moans in the heat
of a summer, come late
with a vengeance.

2 a.m.
and allover the city
bodies sweat
and tingle, the wearers
dancing, wending home,
or fast un asleep.

happiness

lying in bed ofa weekdaymorning
Autumn
and the trees
none the worse for it.
Youve just got up
to make tea toast and a bottle
leaving pastures warm
for me to stretch into

in his cot
the littlefella
outsings the birds

Plenty of honey in the cupboard.
Nice.

the picture

In the Art Gallery it is nearly
closingtime. Everybody has left ex
cept a man and a younggirl
who are gazing at a picture
of themselves. Lifesize and life
like it could almost be a
mirror. However it is not a
mirror, because in a few minutes
a bell will ring and the man
and the younggirl will move
away leaving the original couple
staring into the empty space
provided by this   poem.

the power of poets

the man on the veranda
outside, giving coppers
to the old tramp and
feeling good isn't me.
I am the veranda.
I could have been
the tramp or even
the coppers. However
I choose to be the
veranda and it is
my poem. Such is
the power of poets.

the most unforgettable character i've ever met gives advice to the young poet

GIVE POETRY A BAD NAME

May your poems run away from home
and live between the lines.
May they break and enter, assault and batter,
and loiter in the mind with intent.
May they invite the critics for dinner
and leave before the main course.
May they put a hand up the Muses skirt
(only to find Robert Graves hand already there).
May the dying be anointed with them
and the living vaccinated against them.
May they walk in our sleep
and talk while we are talking.
May they leave understains on the memory.

CREEP UP ON POETRY WHILE SHE'S FEEDING THE DUCKS

May your poems run riots
and sit outside courts where Justice has grown flabby
May they exceed the brain limit
and never stop for hitchhikers.
May they stick in the craw of the law
and fly in the face of gifthorses.
May they bushwack bandwagons
then take to the hills.
May they break new wind.

WHILST RAPING POETRY KEEP HER AT ARM'S LENGTH

(you will thus be more easily identified later).
May your poems save us.
Save us from those who peddle pornography
and who are not sensual.

Save us from those who screw in front of our children.
Save us from those who would replace God
with an autographed picture of themselves.
Save us from those who think they should lead
because they have followers.
Save us from those who think they should lead
because they *want* followers.
Save us from those who think they are right.
Save us from those who think *you* are right.

WHEN POETRY SCREAMS AT YOU THREATEN TO TAKE UP PAINTING

May your poems act their rage
and cry out against the wilderness you have chosen.
May they spit blood into the wind
and once written, seldom regain consciousness.
May they close their eyes and walk in the dark.
May they brandish themselves in undreamed chasms
like a blindman's stick.
May they be seen and heard.
May they ask the unaskable.
Question the unquestionable.
Eke out the unekeoutable
May they ring from the rafters
Live happy ever afters.
May they be damned, and published.

the identification

So you think its Stephen?
Then I'd best make sure
Be on the safe side as it were.
Ah, theres been a mistake. The hair
you see, its black, now Stephens fair ...
Whats that? The explosion?
Of course, burnt black. Silly cf me.
I should have known. Then lets get on.

The face, is that the face I ask?
that mask of charred wood
blistered, scarred could
that have been a child's face?
The sweater, where intact, looks
in fact all too familiar.
But one must be sure.

The scoutbelt. Yes thats his.
I recognise the studs he hammered in
not a week ago. At the age
when boys get clothes-conscious
now you know. Its almost
certainly Stephen. But one must
be sure. Remove all trace of doubt.
Pull out every splinter of hope.

Pockets. Empty the pockets.
Handkerchief? Could be any schoolboy's.
Dirty enough. Cigarettes?
Oh this can't be Stephen.
I dont allow him to smoke you see.
He wouldn't disobey me. Not his father.
But thats his penknife. Thats his alright.

And thats his key on the keyring
Gran gave him just the other night.
Then this must be him.

I think I know what happened
. . . . . . about the cigarettes
No doubt he was minding them
for one of the older boys.
Yes thats it.
Thats him.
Thats our Stephen.

out of sequence

A task completed everyday
keeps sin and boredom both at bay
is what his mother used to say.

In a shop doorway
at the back of Skelhorne St.
a man in his early forties
grinning and muttering
is buttering a piece of bacon
with a pair of rusty scissors.
They are only nail scissors
and he has difficulty holding them
in his clumsy, larded hands.

The next day will be spent
untying the little knots.

In Renshaw Street
a man with blue eyes
and skin the colour of worn pavements
burrows into the busstop litterbin.
The sherrybottle is empty
but there is a bacon rasher
and a screwedup foil of Lurpak
as well as a deflated ball of string

string is great.
It ties up pillowends
and keeps the wind
out of your trouserlegs.
Things dont get lost
when there's string about.
Good to play with in bed.
Always keep some handy.

Near Windsor Street
where they are pulling down houses
there is much that rusts and glistens.
A pair of nail scissors
halfhidden by tin cans, stands,
one foot in the grave.
Approaching is a man
tying a rosary of knots into a length of dirty string.

His life, like this poem,
out of sequence,
a series of impressions,
unfinished, imperfect.

ONCE I LIVED IN CAPITALS
MY LIFE INTENSELY PHALLIC

but now i'm sadly lowercase
with the occasional *italic*

6